Quiet Thoughts

Quiet Thoughts

Reflections on the Meaning of Life

With Photographic Illustrations
by Dr. John C. Weaver

Edited by Ben W. Whitley

 Hallmark Crown Editions

Set in Diotima

Designed by William Hunt

Copyright © 1971 by Hallmark Cards, Inc.,

Kansas City, Missouri. All Rights Reserved.

Printed in the United States of America.

Library of Congress Catalog Card Number: 73-145809.

Standard Book Number: 87529-199-6.

Quiet Thoughts

Write on your hearts that every day
is the best day of the year.

Ralph Waldo Emerson

SEARCH OUT JOY

Never mind pleasure. Search out joy. Pleasure is its shadow. But joy is real, a secret splendor running through all creation.

Like gold, it doesn't lie about the streets waiting to be picked up. It has to be dug for, with diligence and passion. It's in people, to be found through the practice of love. It's in work, in the rigorous exercise of powers of mind or body or spirit. It's a gift the created world is perpetually offering; the price of it is untiring attention to the present moment. It is to be found always and only in the contemplation of reality.

Hunt it down, pursue it, track it to its lair where it dwells. Not in pleasures and pastimes, distractions, piled-up satisfactions, and busyness. It dwells in truth, and nowhere else.

That's why it matters. It will show you moment by moment where truth is for you. And when you know that, cleave to it, turn not aside, be given up to that. That, if you will, is a way of life worth living.

Fae Malania

In the mountains of truth you never climb in vain.

Friedrich Nietzsche

To know the truth is easy; but, ah,
how difficult to follow it.

From the Chinese

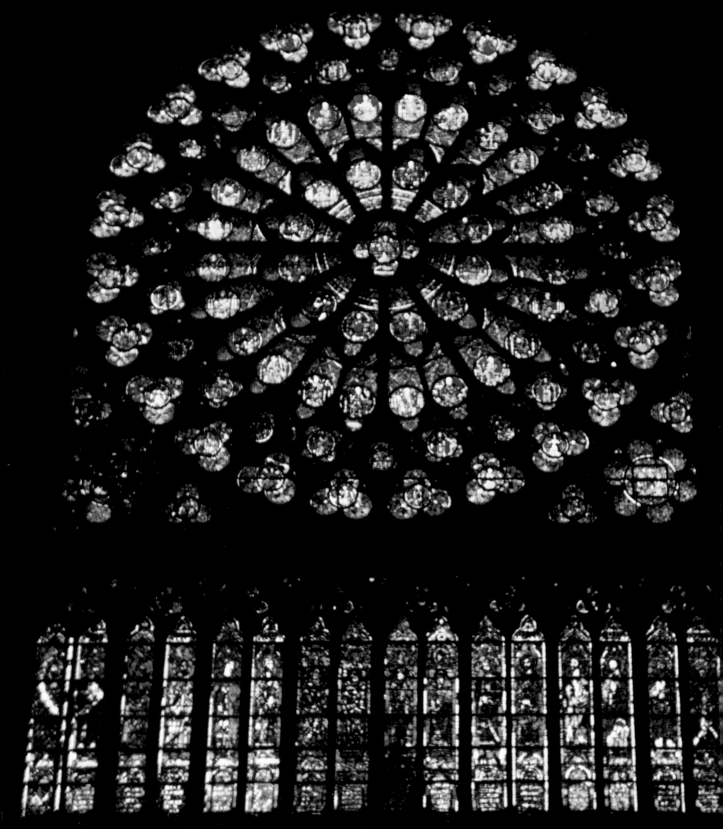

PSALM 95: A PSALM OF GOD'S GREATNESS

O come, let us sing unto the Lord; let us make a
joyful noise to the rock of our salvation.
Let us come before his presence with thanksgiving, and
make a joyful noise unto him with psalms.
For the Lord is a great God, and a great King above all
gods.
In his hand are the deep places of the earth: the
strength (heights) of the hills is his also.
The sea is his, and he made it: and his hands formed
the dry land.
O come, let us worship and bow down: let us kneel
before the Lord our maker.

Nothing in life is to be feared.
It is only to be understood.

Marie Curie

In this my green world
Flowers birds are hands
They hold me
I am loved all day
All this pleases me
I am amused
I have to laugh from crying
Trees mountains are arms
I am loved all day.

Kenneth Patchen

I discovered the secret of the sea
in meditation upon a dewdrop.

Kahlil Gibran

To me every hour of the light
and dark is a miracle.
Every cubic inch of space
is a miracle.

Walt Whitman

What is beautiful is a joy for all seasons
and a possession for all eternity.

Oscar Wilde

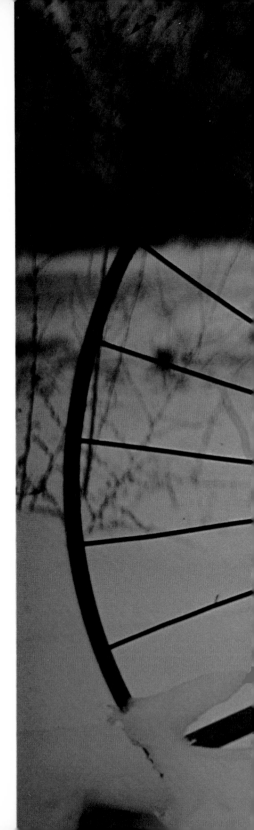

Everything
   has been thought of before,
   but the difficulty
   is to think of it again.

   Johann Wolfgang von Goethe

Who can doubt that we exist only to love?
We live not a moment exempt from its influence.

Blaise Pascal

The journey of a thousand miles begins with a single step.

Lao-Tse

The blue of heaven is larger than the clouds.

Elizabeth Barrett Browning

When I heard
the church bells ring
I thought I heard
the voice of God.

Albert Schweitzer

Ask, and it shall be given you; seek, and ye shall find;
knock, and it shall be opened unto you.

Matthew 7:7

I keep my ideals,
   because in spite of everything
   I still believe that people
   are really good at heart.

Anne Frank

Silence is the perfectest herald of joy:
   I were but a little happy,
   if I could say how much.

William Shakespeare

Far away there in the sunshine are my highest aspirations.
I may not reach them, but I can look up and see their
beauty, believe in them, and try to follow where they lead.

Louisa May Alcott

A COSMOS, NOT A CHAOS

I paused to listen to the silence. My breath
crystallized as it passed my cheeks, drifted on
a breeze gentler than a whisper. The wind vane
pointed toward the South Pole. Presently the
wind cups ceased their gentle turning as the
cold killed the breeze. My frozen breath hung
like a cloud overhead.

The day was dying, the night was being born—
but with great peace. Here were the imponderable
processes and forces of the cosmos, harmonious
and soundless. Harmony, that was it! That was
what came out of the silence — a gentle rhythm,
the strain of a perfect chord, the music of the
spheres, perhaps.

It was enough to catch that rhythm, momentarily
to be myself a part of it. In that instant
I could feel no doubt of man's oneness with
the universe. The conviction came that that
rhythm was too orderly, too harmonious, too
perfect to be a product of blind chance — that,

therefore, there must be purpose in the whole
and that man was part of that whole and not an
accidental offshoot. It was a feeling that
transcended reason; that went to the heart of
man's despair and found it groundless. The
universe was a cosmos, not a chaos; man was as
rightfully a part of that cosmos as were the
day and night.

Admiral Richard E. Byrd

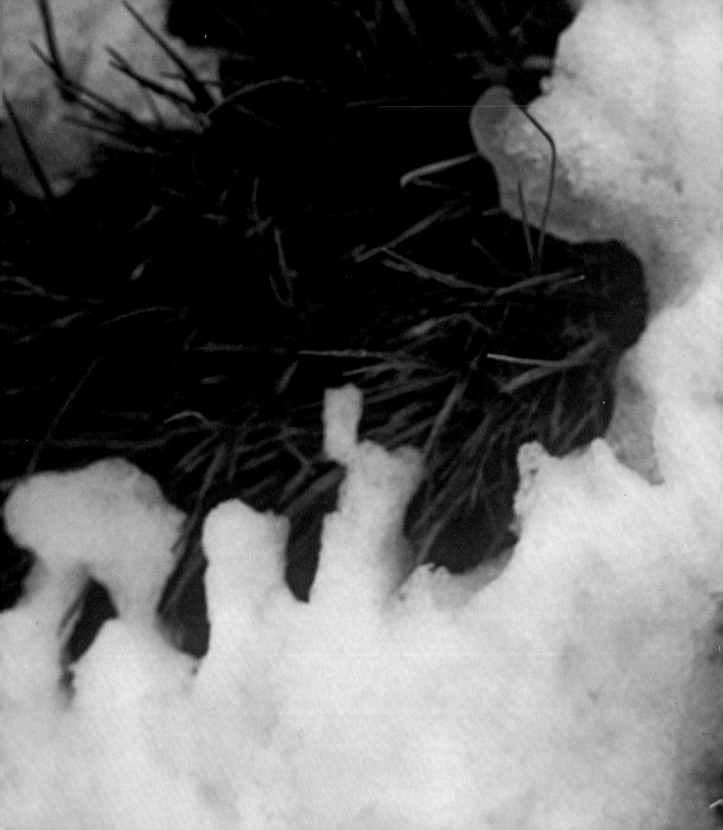

I n the midst of winter, I finally learned
that there was in me an invincible summer.

Albert Camus

...It is only important to love the world...
to regard the world and ourselves and all
beings with love, admiration and respect.

Hermann Hesse

It is necessary for me to see the first point of light which begins to be dawn. It is necessary to be present alone at the resurrection of Day, in the blank silence when the sun appears. In this completely neutral instant I receive from the Eastern woods, the tall oaks, the one word "Day," which is never the same. It is never spoken in any known language.

Thomas Merton

Is it so small a thing
  To have enjoyed the sun,
  To have lived light in the spring,
  To have loved,
  To have thought,
  To have done?

Matthew Arnold

Climb the mountains and get their good tidings. The winds will blow their own freshness into you, and the storms their energy, while cares will drop away from you like the leaves of Autumn.

John Muir

FRAMED IN SPACE

One cannot collect all the beautiful shells on the beach. One can collect only a few, and they are more beautiful if they are few. Gradually one discards and keeps just the perfect specimen. One sets it apart by itself, ringed around by space—like the island.

For it is only framed in space that beauty blooms. Only in space are events and objects and people unique and significant—and therefore beautiful. Even small and casual things take on significance if they are washed in space, like a few autumn grasses in one corner of an Oriental painting, the rest of the page bare.

Anne Morrow Lindbergh

Something to do, someone to love, and something
to hope for, are the true essentials of a happy
and meaningful life.

David Goodman

Nature is the art of God.

Dante Alighieri

Life has loveliness to sell,
All beautiful and splendid things....

Sara Teasdale

If I keep a green bough in my heart,
the singing bird will come.

Chinese Proverb

No bird soars too high,
   if he soars with his own wings.

William Blake

Only that day dawns to which we are awake.
There is more day to dawn.
The sun is but a morning star.

Henry David Thoreau

I have always felt that the moment when first you wake up in the morning is the most wonderful of the 24 hours. No matter how weary or dreary you may feel, you possess the certainty that, during the day that lies before you, absolutely anything may happen. And the fact that it practically always doesn't, matters not one jot. The possibility is always there.

Monica Baldwin

Even if I knew that tomorrow the
world would go to pieces,
I would still plant my apple tree.

Martin Luther

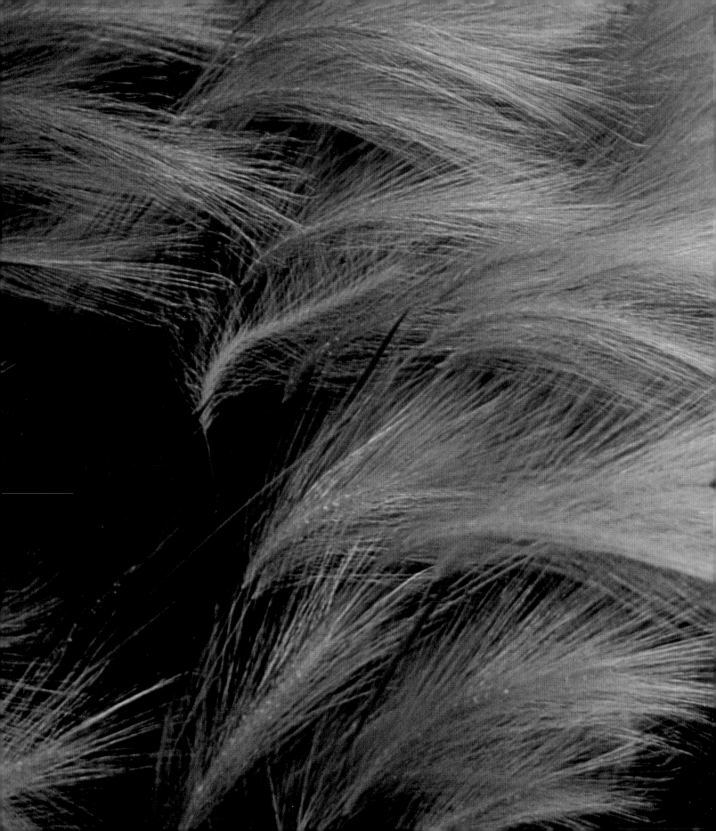